Starting Out for the Difficult World

Other Books by Robert Dana

POETRY

In a Fugitive Season, 1980
The Power of the Visible, 1971
Some Versions of Silence, 1967

PROSE

Against the Grain:
Interviews with Maverick American Publishers, 1986

LIMITED EDITIONS

Blood Harvest, 1986
What the Stones Know, 1982
In a Fugitive Season, 1979
Journeys from the Skin, 1966 (pamphlet)
The Dark Flags of Waking, 1964
My Glass Brother and Other Poems, 1957 (pamphlet)

Starting Out
for the Difficult World

ROBERT DANA

PERENNIAL LIBRARY
Harper & Row, Publishers, New York
Cambridge, Philadelphia, San Francisco, Washington
London, Mexico City, São Paulo, Singapore, Sydney

Poems in this book have appeared in the following magazines: *Another Chicago Magazine:* "Blue Run," "I'm Lucky," "Wichita," "Thaw," "To a Cockroach"; *The American Poetry Review:* "Notre Dame de Paris, 1974"; *The Ark:* "Tanka"; *The Des Moines Register:* "Blood Harvest," "They Know the Beautiful Are Risen"; *The Georgia Review:* "Watching the Nighthawk's Dive"; *Harvard Magazine:* "I Used to Think So"; *The Iowa Review:* "Bad Heart," "Everything Else You Can Get You Take," "Victor"; *Kansas Quarterly:* "Starting Out for the Difficult World"; *Midwest Quarterly:* "Ark & Covenant," "Burn," "On a View of Paradise Ridge from a Rented House," "Written in Winter"; *Mississippi Review:* "New Snow at Goodlove's Grave"; *New England Review:* "Driving the Coeur D'Alene Without You," "Luck," "What the Stones Know"; *New Letters:* "All This Way," "Bread," "Mineral Point," "Transferences"; *Ploughshares:* "Getting It Right"; *Poetry:* "At the Vietnam War Memorial, Washington, D.C."; *Poetry East:* "My Kind"; *Poetry Now:* "Angels & Deaths in St. Augustine," "Key West: Looking for Hemingway"; *Stand* (England): "Blue Run"; *The New Yorker:* "A Short History of the Middle West," "Mnemosyne"; *The North American Review:* "Ninety-One in the Shade"; *The Spirit That Moves Us:* "Horses."

Some of these poems also appeared in limited editions from the Seamark Press, and the Windhover Press of the University of Iowa. This work was supported by a grant from the National Endowment for the Arts.

FIRST EDITION

Designer: Sidney Feinberg

Copyeditor: Karen McDermott

Library of Congress Cataloging-in-Publication Data

Dana, Robert, 1929–
   Starting out for the difficult world.

   I. Title.
PS3554.A5S7   1987   811'.54   87-203
ISBN 0-06-055094-5   87 88 89 90 91 MPC 10 9 8 7 6 5 4 3 2 1
ISBN 0-06-096197-X (pbk.)   87 88 89 90 91 MPC 10 9 8 7 6 5 4 3 2 1

For Phil and Eddie, and Larry
all of them, everywhere

I was black once—when I was poor

LARRY HOLMES

Contents

Horses : 9

IV. WHAT THE STONES KNOW

V. A SHORT HISTORY OF THE MIDDLE WEST

Horses

Horses of earth
Horses of water
Great horses of grey cloud

A blizzard of horses

Dust
and the ponies of dust
Horses of muscle and blood

Chestnuts Roans Blacks
Palominos
Wild dapple of Appaloosas

Spanish ponies
Cow ponies
Broncs Mustángs
Arabians Morgans Tennessee Walkers
Trotters
Shetlands
Massive matched Percherons

Horses
and the names of horses
Whirlaway Man O' War Coaltown
Cannonero
Foolish Pleasure

9

Horses with tails of smoke
The giddy laughter of horses

Horses of war
their necks clothed in thunder
nostrils wide

The ground beneath them
terrible to look on

Horses of anger
Horses of cruelty
wringing the iron bit in their mouths

The horses of Psyche

Blake's horses
The horses of instruction
Horses of breath

Dawn horses

And the one horse in the heart

that runs
and runs

I.

STARTING OUT FOR
THE DIFFICULT WORLD

Starting Out for the Difficult World

This morning, once again,
I see young girls with
their books and clarinets
starting out for the difficult
world. The wind has turned
into the north. It picks a few
leaves from the trees, leaves
already curled, some brown.
They scatter. Even so, their
circles under maple and hack-
berry thicken. The light,
clean as juice to the taste.

Great art, someone said,
rides on the backs of the poor.
Perhaps that's so. But this
is not Long Island. No packed
white waves leap yelping on the shore.
Here, the nights are cold and starry.
Three solitary clouds pig along
the near horizon. And you could
mistake this autumn for Keats's
or your own, or the
autumn of someone you once knew.

Luck

Down the dark day
rain bristles like shaven steel

Bitch-teeth
grinding in him at the bone

Ulcering his flesh
like hooks

until he roars and bleeds

Down on all fours
in a split-footed panicky shuffle

Or singing out
in the razor shriek of pigs in a stock truck

But one day
he'll die into the bright horse of his anger

And white-eyed

splintering with his hooves
the fire-flaked siding

break out

through the slit in his belly
past the surgeon's knife

mane and tail
streaming with flame into the windy dark

In the smoking morning

luck

And the hound
baring its teeth among the blackened stones

The maple leaves
flushed and burning

fallen from a heaven of trees

I Used to Think So

The long sigh of steam through pipes,
the air beyond the window, pearly.

                                    Net-
works of stripped branches, and a shag
of spruce.

Upstairs, my heavy colleague
falls toward what monstrousness of flesh?
When a file drawer rumbles shut,
what righteousness closes on itself?

These are the committees
that grind the heart to powder.

As she leaves,
and the door jerks to a close,
I listen hard into the stillness,
into the building's actual weather,

hearing nothing that loves me,

as if each detail
had to be tricked into meaning.

Outside,
dusk has become reflexive.

The fall of an apple
is the fall of everything,

the sin of gravity.

Seeds, leaves, the child
tumbling from the womb, waterfall and rainfall,
lightfall,

the foot on the stair . . .

What is it once heard
that will not come back in an act of memory

in which the day is as soiled
as the glass of these institutional windows
facing the passion of trees?

To lose it.
Perhaps that's the whole idea after all.

Not to stand
months hence
caught in the doorway of a blue photograph looking strange.

I want to start over again
every day of my life.

Do I?
I used to think so.

I'm Lucky

Sub-zero.
And the birds have lost their talent
for the air.

Back yards
blank with snow. Drifted.
Trampled.

The breath of trees
stripped bare.

My neighbor's blue Maverick
deafens, blind and hub-deep,

on exactly the same spot
he parked it last September.

This wind could cut glass,
freeze your finger to your cheek.

My life is not important.

I understand that.

New Snow at Goodlove's Grave

You walk out

into yourself
into the sub-freezing cold

the heart
that life-pumping murderous muscle numb
body

numb

hands thick as paws
in their double mittens

The snow is blue
the night sky clear

And bitter
against some woman's bitterness

you feel
only your own confusion

turning about you
like flakes

separate stars

wobbling
in their unforgivable orbits

At St. Mary's
the stones of the dead
rise into the light

houses

all dark but one

where a candle
burns so steadily
you do not believe it

behind red glass

And footprints

mouths
gaping and dark with lamentation
choir the deep snow

Reading the name
cut so cleanly into the stone
you believe it

you believe it

your thighs
your face

burning now with the cold

Thaw

You've hoarded it all winter
like a crust of ice.
                              Like thaw.
And spoken to no one.
A few distant friends by phone.
One or two of the great dead
whose pages tell you that,
after our deaths, those we love
lose our names for them, that
disburdened, cleansed, they grow
lighter. The son, the daughters,
—what a relief for them!
Even mornings return to their
original nature. Rain silking
the air. Dandelions strewing
the lawns like butter coins.

You want to die at the edge.

Not here,
where only the young die young.
And the grey dissolving evening
glides easily
into the hands and arms and bodies
of the trees.

All This Way

On a painting by Edward Levine

We have come all this way

to an old leather jacket
nailed by its shoulders
to the wall

its scuff
oiled by the sweat of too many hands

The creases the crush

the three plain buttons
that let the front swing open
tell us nothing

tell us it's the kind of jacket
a man might die in

a flag stuffed in one sleeve
in the other dust

Where the lungs were
that hungered for the whip of saw grass
or burned with the mists of industrial chemicals

where the heart pounded

there is only a blue field
a handful of blurred stars

The belly is a tatter
of red-and-white bunting
The fist a stump of cloth

Where the head would be
with its marvellous eyes
that loved the roundness of a woman

that saw his daughters
filling out
their first white dresses

that flashed to his boy
banging dirty heels
against the pressed tin of the porch

there
there is only intense darkness

A full pink paper rosebud
its wire stem uncoiling
falls across the left lapel

like a rose of breath

Its color seems to bleed
into the grey wall

washing into it

until we can imagine
the mornings and evenings of our fathers

yours and mine
who were killed early

and who left us these walls
to which they pressed their cheeks

the cheap rooms of their lives
each day
emptying and filling with this light

Getting It Right

Lightning cracks its red
and green and violet whips,
or sets its white hooks
deep into your soundest sleep,
and you wake.

                  Four a.m.
Towers of air, dark
glaciers you imagine them,
lurch together, avalanching,
rumbling forward under
earth and sill. Rain
scours down in bushels,
or pops off your windows
like a spray of gravel.

Perhaps you get up then,
and let the cat in,
pausing in the unreal flash
to watch the shocked clothes-
line dance and twitch,
trees bucking and blowing
like burnt nerves.

Perhaps you rinse
from the Roumanian crystal
beside the sink

the dark red seal
of last night's wine.

You want to do the next thing right.
You want the storm to go on.
You want it to rain for days
in the avenues of grey churches,
into your hard arms,
as you sleep, and wake, and sleep.

II.

NINETY-ONE
IN THE SHADE

Mnemosyne

Baryshnikov remembers
a sunny day in Latvia

Holding on to his mother's dress
which is chiffon
with yellow and purple flowers

remembers her ash-blond hair
her bright blue eyes

    *

The escape artists
are identical twins

and remember each other

    *

The three-year-old boy says
"It was red

And very cold"

    *

Susan Hansford
summered on Lake Michigan

Her father
afraid of storms
would often embrace her as the clouds darkened

repeating
"How beautiful" "How beautiful"

    *

A trap springs
in the rat-infested grapes

Harry's fingers ribbon with blood

I remember Harry
sweet drunken Harry

Mineral Point

These immigrant houses
full of clear dry light
face north and east

toward the vanished mouth of the mine

Dressed limestone
And a clear spring
that flows to the kitchen door

where we are told
by a girl whose face
shines like milk

how these Cornish miners
were windlassed by twos
in a wooden bucket

eighty feet down

to drift tunnels
and hack out lead and dry-bone
by candlelight

We have nothing
to love them for

Nothing to forgive

They grew humpbacked

And ate and drank
from tin pails filled with pasty
and water for hot tea

Perhaps they loved their wives

The night
that tumbled down the shafts to them
from Shake Rag St.

like a handful of coin

was the same darkness
that finds us all
naked under our clothes

the same darkness
that chattered beside them
like a stub of black candle

like the starling
in its wicker cage

Ninety-One in the Shade

It's not enough to be good . . .
—James Baldwin

1.

It's always the same

These swelters of brick or boards
The humid tons of air
Metallic breath of ancient drains

In the kitchen
flies cruise the centuries of unwashed dishes
Cops cruise the streets

Your third floor Thirties apartment
taken for space and sleeping porches
decays visibly month by month

But your green plants thrive
in this north light

And the moon of your white face
is still beautiful

2.

After supper
we walk to the bakery
for rolls and black strong bread

or to the laundromat
where our colors gasp and collapse like
television
in the rented glass
of washer doors

The neighborhood
sweats on its dark stoops

Teasing
or pussy-maddened
or weirdo delinquent junkies on a glassy high

In the occasional swing
of headlights
the features of an obscene photograph

where feeling
is the jagged edge of thought

the body
all that keeps us alive

3.
Dead black
of morning

And we wake
to the rich burn of ozone
and the distant low batteries of thunder

Lightning
freaks the roaches

from the bedroom floor

I tell you
how sometimes I imagine myself
an enemy soldier

Summer storms
as artillery shelling the city

Naked on the bed

we talk about
whether you think of yourself
as beautiful

about your girlhood

your older sister
who is unhappy

The rain has begun to fall

Clicking in the leaves
beside the window

Puddling the rutted alleys

Then
whistling through the screens
scouring the sills

it monsoons
into the empty streets

cold and foot-wringing

until our windows blur
like the stunned windows in a dream

the endless succession of rented rooms
in which nobody lives

    4.
Along del Mar
seven days a week

the jag of gas-blue ghost-green letters
and girls

hot-nippled in neon
sizzling on then off then on

Spelling it out

Strain your gut
in the sheep-kill forever

You will never
own a house on the water

Or under the green trees
where time passes quickly

and the wings of butterflies
are dusted a delicate blue

5.

Our last morning together
you sit on the edge of the bed
stroking a vein in your thigh

Your hair
smells of coffee and eggs

If I kiss you
you will cry

In a vacant lot
where the baked earth blinks with the mercy
of broken glass

a small black boy
tries to get his tail-less kite
to fly

The three of us
tie the rag of my handkerchief to it

And watch it
haul at its saddle-string

tugging the live sail of its colors up
into the hot gust

like a word remembered

that we do not say

Blue Run

Maxie's Golden Garden Bar
where gorgeous mommies disco
in a glass box, and you tell me
how tough it is—kissing ass
at Harvard and cashing Daddy's
checks. How the best is none
too good, and you're lonely.

Why is it *my* life you think
you want on a dust jacket?
Poetry never saved anyone.

My mother—Dietrich-faced,
Hollywood, Anglo-Irish angel—
died at forty, of pneumonia and
neglect, in rooms above a store.
We were hungry. She was buried
cheap in Roxbury. It was 1934.

Would you move her to richer
ground? Weep for her? Set above
the rack and broken fever of
her bones, marble to give off
light brighter than a star?

And what the hell would you do
with my sister? For whom each day

became one long, frightened prayer.
And God, a black habit. Can you
mend her orphan's wheedle?

I give you the hand-me-downs,
every old man's shirt I hated,
the shoes that never fit.
And the scorched breath of fields
where I bent and chopped tobacco
until my arms went numb, and my
chest, ribs showing through,
blackened with bitter tar.

It's not for everyone,
                the drink
of water lifted in the hands:
face wrinkling in the breath,
disappearing—twining, dwindling
between the fingers: sift, pale
oils, invisible codes of salt
dissolving in the blue run and
molten sunlight of the Charles.

Bread

for E. L. Mayo, 1904–1979

Not Wonder in its white wrapper
with yellow, red, and blue balloons,
or Colonial, or Sunbeam,
those breads of air
you can accordion down to a slice,
limp cake that won't
take peanut butter without tearing,
a cheap cloth of crust. No.

Real bread.
Its crumb tight,
grist for cheese, *wurst,* or hard sausage,
a mop to thick, steaming soups;
braided loaves, or long French ones
to be cut with a pocket knife,
or rounds with gashed tops,
grainy, and brown, and water crusted,
with a haze baked on them
you can sink your teeth into.

In that soft ratcheting
of sifter against screen,
any afternoon we can find the time,
we can make ghosts of our hands
in the silk of flour;

and in the beer of yeast,
be sure of the one ingredient necessary

to three risings and kneadings
on the cracked board,
until the greased tins
are finally dusted with granules
of white cornmeal,
and even the sleep of this house
sweetens with this art.

Old Irishman, my father,
you with your Saturday sleeves rolled up,
and smelling powerfully of Lucky Tiger like whiskey—
you knew all about it,
the making of bread.

Transferences

Like a reading of ashes

Like acid rain
    the black motorcycle Kabuki of Kiss

Like this tenement of ice where the first bright spider
    of dusk is threading her net

Like a sad flatfoot
Like spade cats and silken tits flashing on North Wells

Like *8-Pack* and *Novocaine* and *Devil's Deuce*

Like a motel in high drag
    your room darkened to a white envelope on the floor

Like the groan of sleepers under the track

Like St. James Park where the sailcloth of empty deck chairs
    spinnakers in the wind

Manet at Belle Isle the sea foaming on canvas

Like the roar of insects

Like a tumble of geese barking and yelping down the
high dark

stringing out
on the great letters of their instincts

Like cold Canadas of light

At the Vietnam War Memorial, Washington, D.C.

Today, everything takes
the color of the sun. The air
is filed and fine with it;
the dead leaves, lumped
and molten; flattened grass
taking it like platinum;
the mall, the simple, bare
plan of a tree standing
clothed and sudden in its
clean, explicable light.

And across the muddy
ground of Constitution
Gardens, we've come to find
your brother's name, etched
in the long black muster
of sixteen years of war—
the earth walked raw
this morning by workmen still
gravelling paths, and people
brought here by dreams
more solemn than grief.

A kid in a sweater hurries
past us, face clenched
against tears. And couples,
grey-haired, touching hands,

their Midwestern faces calm,
plain as the stencilled names
ranked on the black marble
in order of casualty.
The 57,939 dead. Soldiers,
bag-boys, lost insurance
salesmen, low riders
to nowhere gone no place—
file after broken file
of this army standing at rest.

Were there roses? I can't
remember. I remember
your son playing in the sun,
light as a seed. Beside
him, the names of the dead
afloat in the darker light
of polished stone. Reo
Owens. Willie Lee Baker.
Your brother. The names
of those who believed and
those who didn't, who died
with a curse on their lips
for the mud, the pitiless sea,
mists of gasoline and rain.

In your photograph, it's
1967. June. On the pad
of a carrier, Donald squats
in fatigues, smoking, beside
a rescue chopper, a man
loneliness kept lean;
the sea behind him slurs

like waste metal. He looks
directly at the camera, and
his eyes offer the serious
light of one who's folded
the empty hands of his
life once too often.
Before nightfall, his bird
will go down aslant God's
gaze like a shattered
grasshopper, and the moons
in the paddies cry out
in burning tongues.

All words are obscene
beside these names. In the
morning the polished stone
gives back, we see ourselves—
two men, a woman, a boy,
reflected in grey light,
a dying world among the dead,
the dead among the living.
Down the poisoned Chesapeake,
leaking freighters haul
salt or chemicals. In a grey
room, a child rises in her
soiled slip and pops the
shade on another day; blue,
streaked with high cloud.

These lives once theirs
are now ours. The silver
air whistles into our lungs.
And underfoot, the world

lurches toward noon and
anarchy—a future bright
with the vision of that
inconceivable, final fire-storm,
in which, for one dead second,
we shout our names, cut
them, like these, into air
deeper than any natural
shadow, darker than avenues
memoried in hidden trees.

To a Cockroach

My cockroach,
my companion.
There is no easy way.

I've seen you drowned
in refrigerated butter.

In New York, one April,
touching a kitchen switch,
I flicked ordinary night
into delirium.
          All
your old varieties
dizzying the wall
above the pitch and spill
of mouldering dishes.

Hysteria of survival
riding the light.

It comes on us suddenly.
Too quick to be cold.

I loved a girl once
who slammed you dead by half
dozens, night after night,
in a St. Louis railroad

flat. Her big box
of Ohio Blue Tips making
the cheap table silver
jump and ring. Jesus,
she was beautiful!

But you're the perfect
survivor. Twenty-five
million years of humility.

Let's hear it,
tiny jewels of typhoid,
for quickness, aliases:
Shiner. Steam Fly. *Peri-
planeta americana.*

*La cucaracha, la cucaracha,
ya no puede caminar . . .*
Drunker than artillery.

That girl I loved
I married. And this morning,
the wind lazy in the window
sheers, sheets rich
with the colors of privilege,
coupled jet fighters
from a nearby air base
sucking everything up,
every word up
into God's roaring void,
I'm giddy.

Cockroach,

companion,
yours is the life that lasts,
the durable low babble.
Your eyes, quick and dark.
Mine, slow and blue.

Notre Dame de Paris, 1974

We give them up
our cities washed in grit

to the whispers of the skin

All but Paris
our grey nun

making a revolution of the rain

a gargoyle
lifting up its stone wing
as if it were an angel's

I see your face
even with my eyes closed

the long banner of your hair

If you would love ugliness
then touch me

Take my anger
to your lips

It will open prisons

It will give a name
to that kiss that spreads its sheer colors

like a bloom of oil
on waters filthy with winter

In the wild belfry
Lady

of this bed

humped and deaf as Quasimodo

ululalia
shaking bone and blood

we ride this ton
of jubilation

banging and banging
together

clapper and bell

Watching the Nighthawk's Dive

Not even a hawk,
but with a hawk's heart
for the dive—

how many years
of dusks have I watched you,
sucker,

fluttering,
as if short of breath,
to a height,

taking aim
on the wing, then plummeting
toward her,

toward soot
stack, schoolhouse roof, or bare
scatter of gravel,

at the last
second, popping the chute,
riding the umbrella-

strutted, down-
curved wings in a humming
skid,

a Jesus dance,
a soft bronx cheer for the void—
then

climbing again
to dive over and over and over
until the first star's gone

and I can only
hear you,
and the streetlights come on.

I could say
I've loved nothing in this whole, dumb country,
and nobody.

But it wouldn't be true,
brown soul.
—I've loved you.

III.

ANGELS

Bad Heart

So you walk along nowhere—
anybody's beach—the air
a rank chowder of low tide
and you're happy. You'd like
to sew yourself a shirt
out of sunlight. You want
to tell your wife you love
her. And you wait for the
telephone in your ear to ring—
For an hour. For a week. Is
abstraction a net or a sieve,
Angel? Is an idea a kiss?
A shape such as maples
make unfurling, or willows
falling? Or a steady river
taking up silt and stone,
showing you in a knot or curl
depth and speed of channel.

And what does it show
if a boat-tail still rudders
in the bucking crosswind of
your head, where you put it
one green Middle-Western
afternoon ten years ago,
when you were younger,
and she was very young?

Key West: Looking for Hemingway

On Mallory Docks
the kids applaud
when the sun goes down

Women
in the hot splash of Key West print

Cayo Hueso

where the light gathers
thick enough to breathe

And up at Southernmost
in his air-conditioned room
an off-duty cop sprawls

cooling
in the bruised blue art of his tattoos
veins shot full of lye

The look of the eyes
you would remember   Papa

And the yellow rice
and the black beans and Cuban bread
at the Miramar

Standing here
knee-deep in the shallows
watching the small wahoo holding steady

ghost-fish

I think of you
with your forehead smashed
into perfect prose

plumbing the blue gulf of the Gulf

Behind the *Pilar*
the marlin
breaks water like a great angel

shaking from its sail
a halo of sun-struck brine

And I call out
silently

in a voice you cannot hear

into that terrible
that clear emptiness

where you were

Angels & Deaths in St. Augustine

for my daughter, Arden

1.

The flat four-pointed star
of the Castillo

rises
low on the edge of the bay

A mile distant
spits of sand the Spaniards and English murdered for

a white wing
cruising the strait

2.

In his tourist surrey
an old man

sits black as slavery
under a silk hat

his stump
under a blanket

You shine beside him
through the shaded streets

Past the city gates
and The Ponce de León palmed in elegant decay

In the narrow
restored lanes

our horse
breathes like starvation

The man's voice
lifts from the gravels of anguish

the story of each place
each improbable day

La Señora
de la leche

and some other history
weary as an old blues

The slave market
passed with a word

we step down
tourists still crowding the promenade

You fix to his lapel
the orange carnation you bought from a Hare Krishna

Radiant
you do not kiss his cheek

3.

Overhead
the sky mackerels

the light of this late December afternoon
is pure

At your feet
the Atlantic ebbs

You stand
in a rubble of shells

tearing
a heel of wheat into pieces

The gulls
flash and cry and wheel about you

And pluck your bread
from the water

On the Public Beach, St. Augustine

Sanderlings. Turnstones. A lone
willet. Fog-colors morning
sun hasn't quite cut through.
The still cold, grey-green March
Atlantic rolling shoreward flank
after glassy flank. Fraying,
plunging, flattening in its final
scouring rush, to salty lager.
Our old *Sylvan*'s gone, with its
blue-shuttered, wind-scrubbed
weekend cabins. Its tiny
kitchenettes. Wind-white
bedsheets rich with the whiff
of something healing. The quick,
illimitable light. Bulldozed
out for a squat of brown condos.
But the beach is still the public
beach we remember. And we follow
its straggling tidelines like kids,
picking among the strew of broken
arks and angel wings and razors.
The sun lags. But I can't wait
to wade out on the water's
electric chill. The skin buzzes.
The young shine like seraphim
just stepped from their clothes.
Remember how each brisk, incoming

breaker caught our breaths
and lifted us to our toes,
until we took a wet shoulder
and rode it in? Up the beach,
somebody's dog barks like heaven,
flinging itself for joy over
the live backs of the waves.
We laugh, and our talk dwindles
to held hands, as if we perceived,
in body, these things, immediate
and whole. As if we lived, as pure
mathematicians say, on a set
of measure zero, where anything
might happen. At Matanzas, south
of here, *jubilatio* at noon:
shrimp fresh-steamed to crispness
at King's Bait and eaten from
a plastic cup, their tails tossed
to the complaining gulls. As if,
far out from shore, four pelicans
might coast, perfectly echeloned,
long crests and spills of light.
The last time we came here,
in '79, Hurly'd just killed
himself, blown his head open,
back in Iowa, with his god-
damned Smith & Wesson,
the brown corn-stubble essing
easy over the winter hills,
like the ancient Chinese character
for river. Now, I no longer
believe we return as birds or fish
or even grit on the heave of the wind.

I think we were never anything
but what we are: the last, lovely,
complex turn of it. And like
the planet, once, and for one
time only. Inventors of this
sea of cloud-struck afternoons,
of heat-haze, the happy dog
of the waves—walking at sunup
with other strangers this flat
reach of sand, and smiling
occasionally back at them
as we pass. Saying, occasionally,
"Good morning. Good morning."

Black Angel

The wind walks past my window again
wearing a dress of green leaves.
I look up. But no one's there.
I'm studying *A Field Guide to Wild-*
flowers. I've just discovered
the tall, spiky ones on my back
slope, the ones with heads of tiny,
pink, rattler mouths, are woodbane,
and it seems to make a difference.
I'm curing herbs. Rose smell
of pepper. Pepper of fresh basil.
And here in the old root cellar
where I write, one good sentence
makes a difference. And Barber's
Adagio for Strings. The opening
of de Boisvallee's *Religioso.*
This poem is an adagio. A slow
yearning of winds and strings.
Like the hot August night I got
drunk with friends, and laughing
and sweating, we linked arms and lay
back in the deep wine, the cool
Einstinian space of summer grass,
streaming upward like angels,
past trees, past crumbling eaves
and stars, rising like music farther
and farther out the closer home.

So I'm checking the rue, the rose-
mary, the sweet marjoram. I'm closing
the book of flowers. All stories
yearn and sing, Rodina Feldevertova,
and that makes a difference.
The parsley will smell of England;
the oregano and basil of Greece;
the rosemary remind us of heaven.
They say you died, mysteriously,
at seventeen, homeward bound
on an Italian liner. Now you stand,
larger than life, over your own grave,
the famous Black Angel of Iowa City,
the iron cape of your wings
spreading its perfect shadow in perfect
sunlight, the right one pointed
upward to protect us, the left
touching the earth, to gather us in.

Now

You come over a hill, suddenly,
late afternoon or early evening
on 6A to Beach Point. Provincetown
to Long Point Light, a yellow,
dissolving Venice by Whistler
or Monet. Bay flat. Silver
grey. Dark blue further out.
I'm not talking about the past.
I'm talking about my sister,
my wife, myself—all of us
travelling without reservations.
I'm talking about three small
sails tacked on the far horizon.
At Shoreline Village, cabins
1930s, sixty bucks a night
and twenty yards from salt water,
my sister talks about shells.
Sister Whine. Sister Twinkle.
Fifty years a nun this spring
and all No to my Yes. A taste
for dull food, and expensive
Irish whiskey in her tea. Next
door, our neighbors play volley-
ball without a net, their little
girls shrieking like seabirds.
Danielle. Michelle. Julie.

I'm not talking about childhood.
I'm saying when the tide here
goes out its long mile at dusk,
the bay's a wet barnyard where
a dozen boats strand and heel over,
and clammers rake the golden muck
for steamers. Later, the years
come down slowly like stars
on Mama's West Dennis or Harwich
or wherever we summered the fall
she died, hundreds of herring-fry
shoaling and sparkling in a bright
terror of shallows, my sister's
beads clicking in the night. I'm
not talking now about memory,
but the way words leap backward
to their beginnings, Wittgenstein's
"significant silences," his desk
drawer of posthumous phrases,
words detached into mystery
on little scraps of blue paper.
So the clear argument of morning
comes on, and lovers rise
from their rented beds to lie
in the sun. In Commercial Street,
one man receives from another
"the signature of God" in his hand.
"What is it?" I ask my wife.
A talisman? A smooth stone?
A word from Hebrew cast in silver?
I lay back on the sand of this
rough prayer of a beach and close

my eyes on the four white ribs
of the sky, listening to the low
roll of surf say *"jour," "jour,"*
and sometimes *"toujours"* to the shore.

IV.

WHAT THE STONES KNOW

What the Stones Know

Fire says
"The flesh. The flesh."

Water says
"Hair."

The air says
one or two feathers in a field of wheat.

Earth says
"Sweat."

The mowing
dazzles with the shadows of passing clouds.

I say to my son,

"Write your name
on everything that's yours."

Driving the Coeur d'Alene Without You

Rain shadows the lake,
and the road curves away and then back,
back and then up, and the sun
appears and disappears.

Below,
the knifetip flash and white wing-dip of mainsails,
the blue of sunburst spinnakers.

In a green fjord,
a canopied motor launch turns the water back
in two icy curls from its prow.

I tell you,
the dumb stain on my shirtpocket
could pass for loneliness.

I want it over quickly.

One by one,
the bays go by: Beauty, Turner, Bell . . .
and long,
dusty constellations of mountain asters.

At Powderhorn,
I pass a family of three
picking berries.

The woman
a print dress in the brambles.
The man hardly glances up.

Their boy stands
stock-still in his faded, dirt-stained T-shirt,
watching me pass,

his eyes solemn with worry
like the eyes
of any young, wild thing.

At Harrison Flats,
the sky is cut by wires, and a combine
dies in a stubblefield.

I am numb.

I drive on
toward the house I live in
that is not mine,

and where,
so that I will never feel shame,
so that I will not dream,

you left
stalked and whiskered heads of wheat
in a ripple-glass pitcher

beside the door.

On a View of Paradise Ridge
from a Rented House

Crest and body
feathered dark with pines,

its wheatstubble right wing
stroking downward,

it holds its slow, hooked
glide toward winter.

A stray hackle of smoke
drifts back, dun and grey,

where a field is burning.
The evening light is dry,

a light that is nothing
that makes all things real.

Behind me, a great
wall of glass trembles.

I can taste my own blood,
strong as coffee,

dark as this furious burgundy.

Written in Winter

The clustered orange
berries of mountain ash
are belled with snow.

The tree itself
templed with winter.

The others, tufted,
boled, and battened.

The most distant,
clouded like a breath
of frozen steam,

the miles of ground
everywhere, zillioned
with crystals.

Here, in the bright
zeroes of this air,
nothing happens.

But later,
your nostrils burn,
your teeth ache.

And all night

you ask the children
of the world

to forgive you.

V.

A SHORT HISTORY
OF THE MIDDLE WEST

A Short History of the Middle West

Under this corn,
these beans,
these acres of tamed grasses,

the prairie still rolls,

heave and trough,
breaker and green curl,

an ocean of dirt tilting and tipping.

Its towns
toss up on the distance, your distance,
like the wink

of islands.

And the sky
is a blue voice
you cannot answer for.

The forked and burning wildflowers
that madden
the ditches

nod without vocabulary.

Your neighbor
is out early this morning—the air
already humid as raw diamond.

Drunk or lonely,
he's scattering large scraps of white
bread for the birds

as if it were winter.

He'd give you the sour undershirt off
his back—
sweet, bad man.

Does he remember
rain salting down from that flat, far shore
of clouds

slowly changing
its story?

On this shore,
the trees all babbling with their hands?

Wichita

If there's no winter here,
it's only for lack of snow.
Take a meadow abandoned to real
estate; the real estate abandoned
to grass and weed; the sky, zinc;
the north wind, iron; and banging,
sliding, down the shadows
of wheel-ruts, down the long
double lane of trees
that lead to no abandoned farm-
house, no tumbled foundations;
the way just stopping dead
at the swampy crossing
where newer tracks cut through.
There, we're left to do
what we can with the hawk
driven off by a crow, the couple
of pines flanked south,
and the rosebush, run wild and
tough in the pale sun, flashing
rose hips bright as any petals.
You get this like a slow post-
card from one of those tropical
countries, the view fixed
in one corner in the window
of the stamp: cheap, exotic, vivid.

Everything Else You Can Get You Take

It's that kind of day.
Hay and panic grass
combed into rolling windrows.
Minstrel-faced sheep. A few
head of crossbred Charlies.

No place we ever imagined
we'd be. No sea's edge
where a low wave sputters,
ignites like a fuse, and races
hissing along the shore.
No thin, viral mist fizzing
the windshield, gorges rising
grey as China in the rain.

Only this long roll of
space where day lilies
leap any breaks in the fences,
flooding down ditches, orange
against the many colors of green—
only the jingle and ring of
morning crickets in the dew.

Don't ask how long we've
been here, or why we stayed.
You fall in love with
a climate. Everything else
you can get you take.

My Kind

My kind? I don't know *my* kind.
I see the sunlight speaking
in the windy leaves—a clear,
cold, early summer day that says
whatever is lost will come down
the daylight to meet you.

Forget it. There's never anyone.
And I find myself wanting
to invent a new language. My
country's the scratch of rain on
glass, these straight miles of
crucified wire—empty as a rose.

Remember the night skies? Navy.
A silk drawn slowly from the
breast pocket for the last deep
trick of the stars: the splash,
the scraps of silver tinselling
down in the flooding white light.

Black Light

Black-light daylight
shadow cat flickering and
shocking her own barred
shadow through shadow
and light, there and not
there, freezing the eye
in a dapple of deadly flowing.

"Tabby" in Arabic
reads "watered silk."

It's late summer, 1985.

And sear. Sear.
Sundown after sundown
the Mississippi glittering like crushed foil.

Now we're walking home,
bringing with us whole
lives of pain as physical
as the bubbling of our small
brown wrens.
                    Thumb-sized
outpourings of brightness—
unbelievable, almost
without end, filling the

empty calligraphy of green
leaves, overwhelming
at last, like evening,
all the wild cherry trees.

Heat

The valley brims with it.
Steamy sea floor
of trees where small birds
swerve and dart like fish.
God's old ocean of grey air,
where a lone crow rows,
slow and steady, toward
home, or nowhere in particular,
on strong, black oars.

True Story

What does the morning say
I wish I hadn't heard before,
the wind still for the first
time in days, the little maple
standing like sodden bronze
beside the garden. Beneath
it, the green roses of the cabbages
unfold, zucchini spread the
canopies of their first true
leaves.
        Tell me again how your
uncle Willie sold his acre
of downtown Wichita for five
bucks and a shot of booze.
And how, where oil-rockers
dipsy-doodle in the wheat,
fire of sex or soul could fry
a young girl's hair to ringlets.

If the rich talk only
to the rich, then it's true:
we are whatever's left of us.
In the scrub, the cardinal
whistling like a rubber mouse.
But nothing's so exotic here
as the emptiness of ordinary
day. It falls through the eyes

of my cat, turning slowly, like
flakes of sunlight in the air.

Blood Harvest

Say "Goodbye." Say whatever
you want. Summer here begins
like thirty years of trying
to breathe under water.
                              Blue
corn surging the plumped lap
and sow-belly hills. Sweat.
Nights rinsed in hot moonlight.

The farmer who looks at you
and crumbs dirt from under
a thumbnail black as cake.

You don't leave it. You
give two fingers to a whirling
gear, your children to the
church. Slash lips and tongue
and arms until blood rains
on the harvest, tasselled and
feathered and green as
the dumb god of the grass.

Prayer in a Time of Murder and Suicide on the Farm

Prince of the rain,

                    it falls on me in tatters.

The sky you don't see is a tall harvest of clouds,
and the air, blue-grey, you don't care about,
marches in on its long, bright stems.

The plain plains burst open Raggedy-Ann raw.

These are the deep dreams deathy at the edges.

This. They say this:

                    Untie the knot of your
face. Open the thrilling fist of your heart.

Victor

A farmhouse left to high
grass. Clapboard grey-
white as wind-scoured bone.
The mouth of the doorway,
the eye of one window
battered shut. So many
stories gibbering in and
out of this empty head
like shadowy small birds.
We see it at 186,000
miles a second, the speed
light travels from even
a vanished star. Victor
out back in his vegetable
garden. His raked and
stained fedora. Scrubbed
knuckles of young potatoes
bubbling up under his hoe.
His woman calls him into
the fading house for supper,
the spider by her window
riding out the wind in its
harness of silk, light in
the trees coming and going.
But Victor stays, watching
the bright air of evening
rain down, bloom, fill.

They Know the Beautiful Are Risen

Old Hog-Eye. Feedlot pig-
god, and back forty eater
of children, snuffles down
the happy mud of heaven,
his great sow swilling it
together with the bright eye
of a butcher weighting scales.
Bacon or sausage. Ham.
Hocks for beans. Pickled
trotters. And years of
being in bad with the Jews.

Is there ice in the glove
in the sty? The wallow
of rich slops for curly
tails and bright tusks
her root eye opens, his stump
of brain shocks and sparks
from juicy channels, exactly
like any other story
that dies each night
when the sky burns down?

Figure it out.
They know the beautiful are risen.

Ark & Covenant

Chip, chirr, blabber, whistle, hingey
squeak
of spring birds.

We all know what that means.

Lawns patched and clotted
with snow.
Shadows and the late sun slanting.

I hardly ever speak
my own language any more.

My mouth fills with silence.

With a useless kiss.

Nothing
to devil the restless ear. Nothing
to sign

on the clear and solemn air.